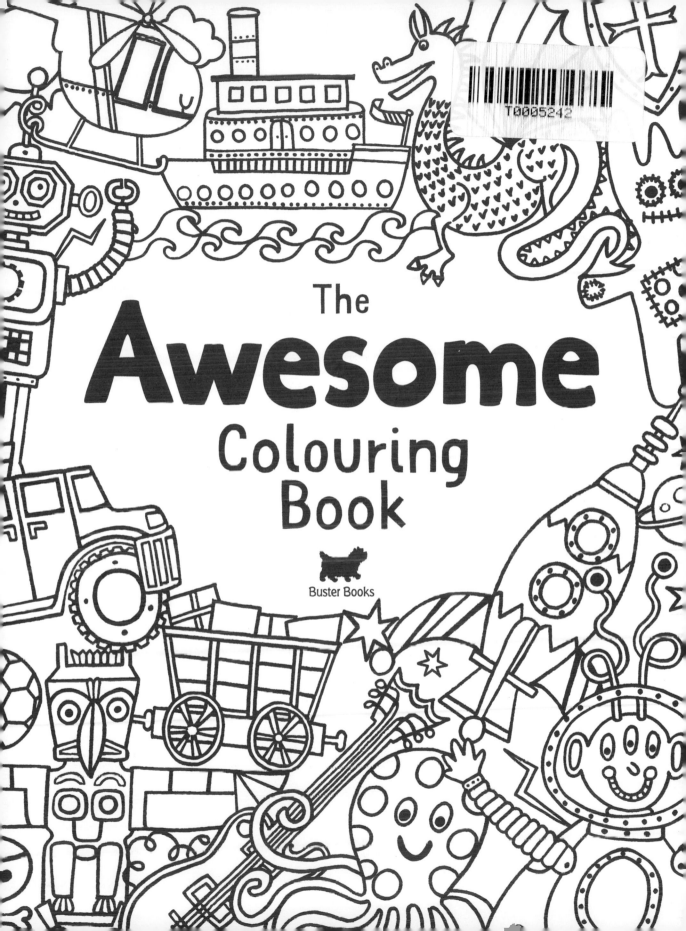

The
Awesome
Colouring
Book

Buster Books

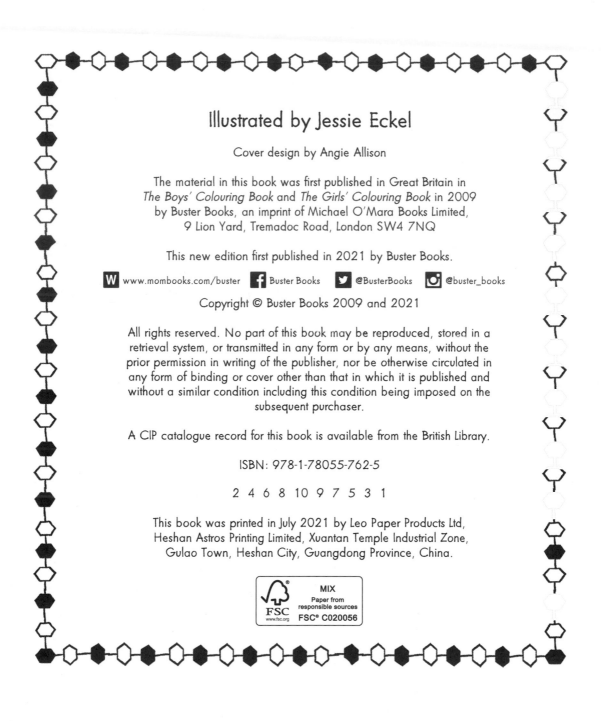

Illustrated by Jessie Eckel

Cover design by Angie Allison

The material in this book was first published in Great Britain in
The Boys' Colouring Book and *The Girls' Colouring Book* in 2009
by Buster Books, an imprint of Michael O'Mara Books Limited,
9 Lion Yard, Tremadoc Road, London SW4 7NQ

This new edition first published in 2021 by Buster Books.

W www.mombooks.com/buster f Buster Books 🐦 @BusterBooks 📷 @buster_books

A CIP catalogue record for this book is available from the British Library.

ISBN: 978-1-78055-762-5

2 4 6 8 10 9 7 5 3 1

This book was printed in July 2021 by Leo Paper Products Ltd,
Heshan Astros Printing Limited, Xuantan Temple Industrial Zone,
Gulao Town, Heshan City, Guangdong Province, China.

MIX
Paper from
responsible sources
FSC® C020056
FSC
www.fsc.org

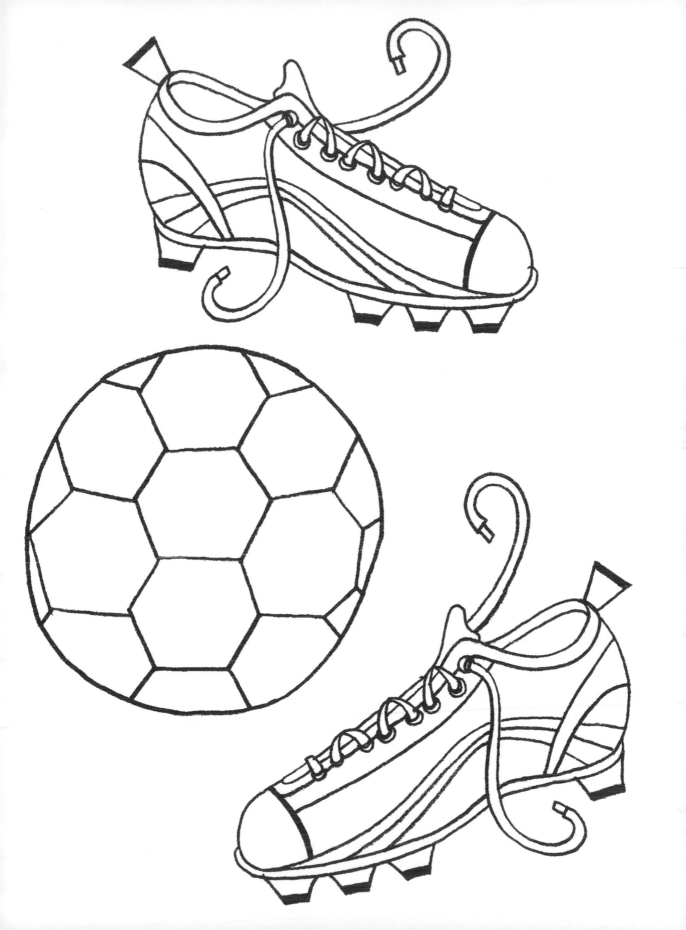

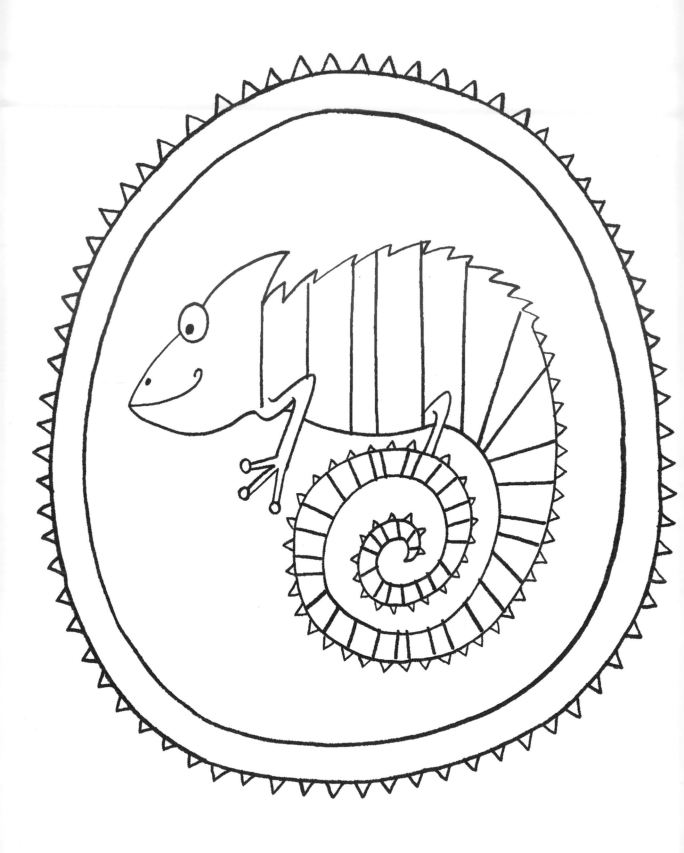

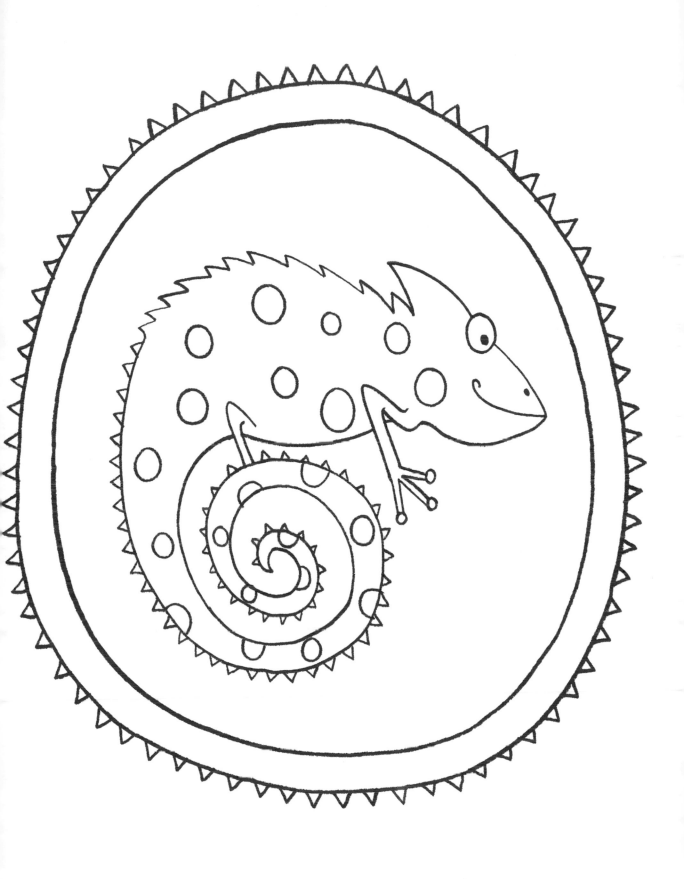

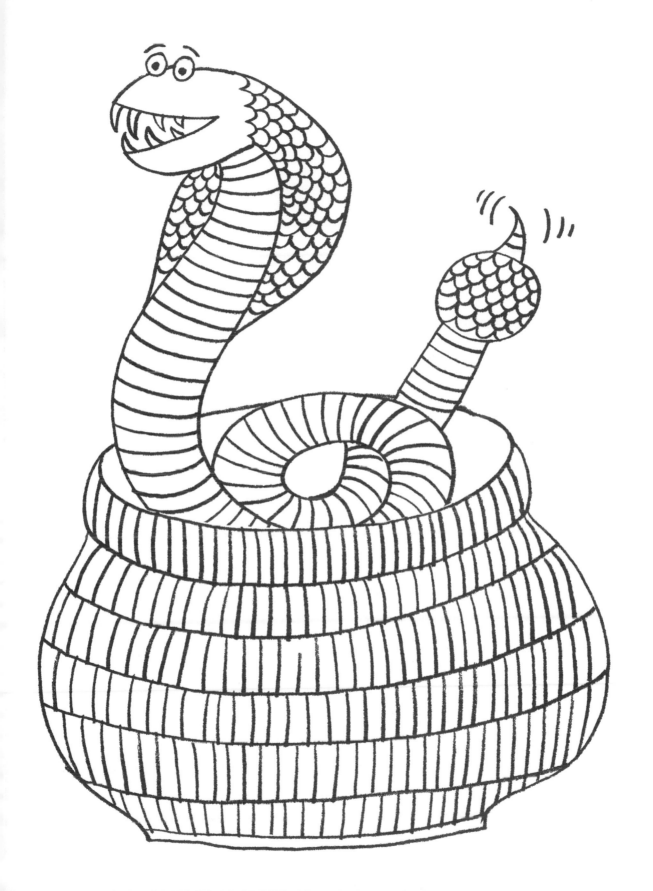

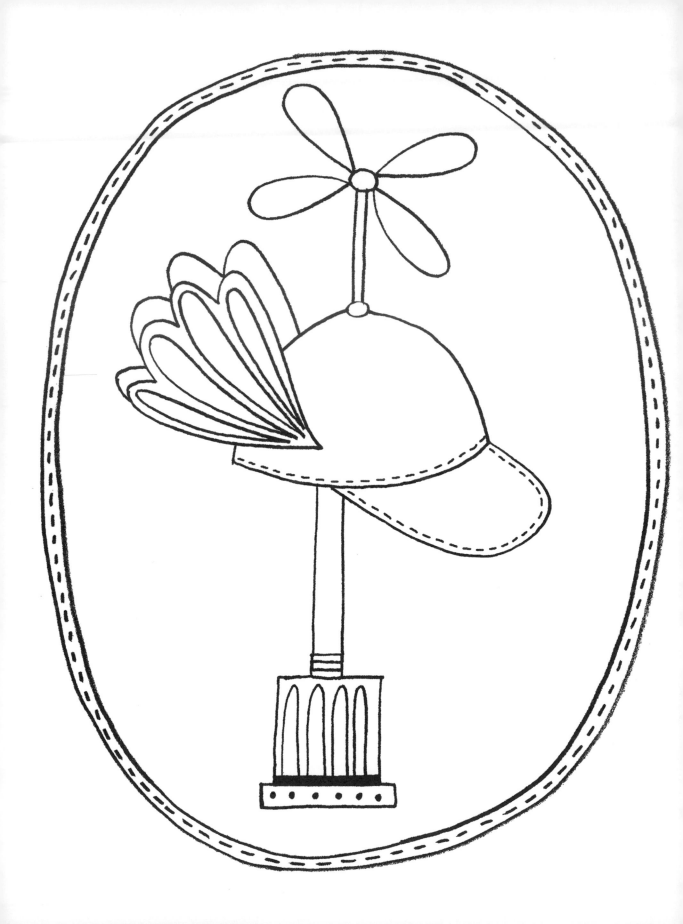

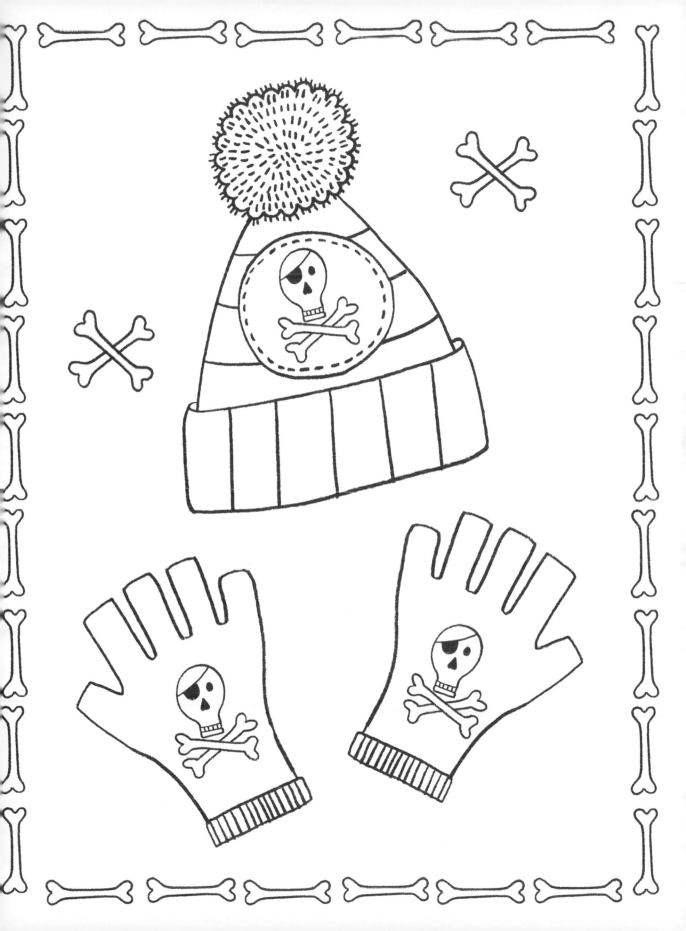

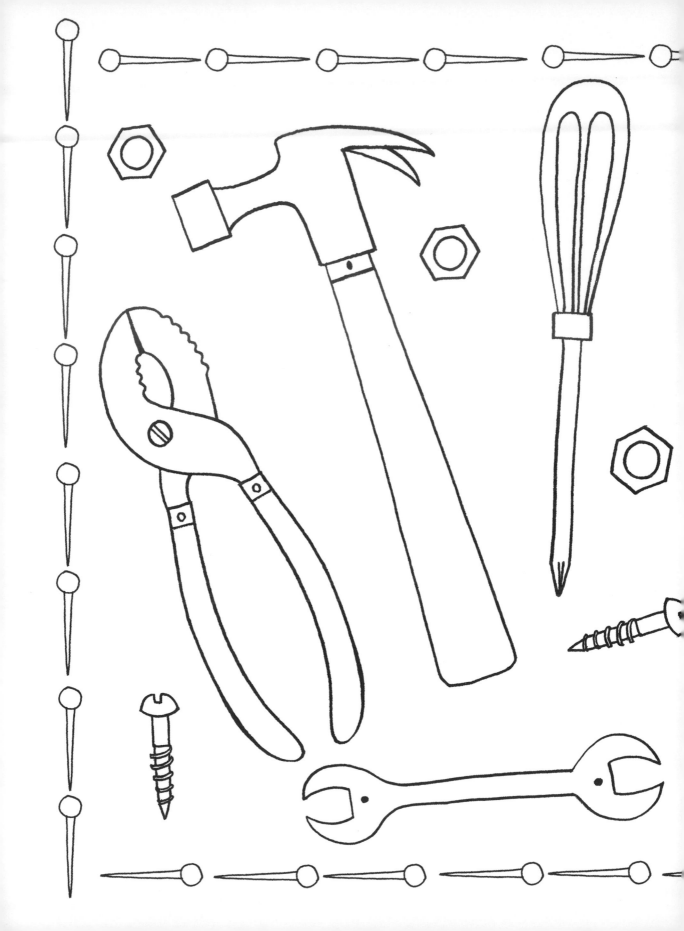

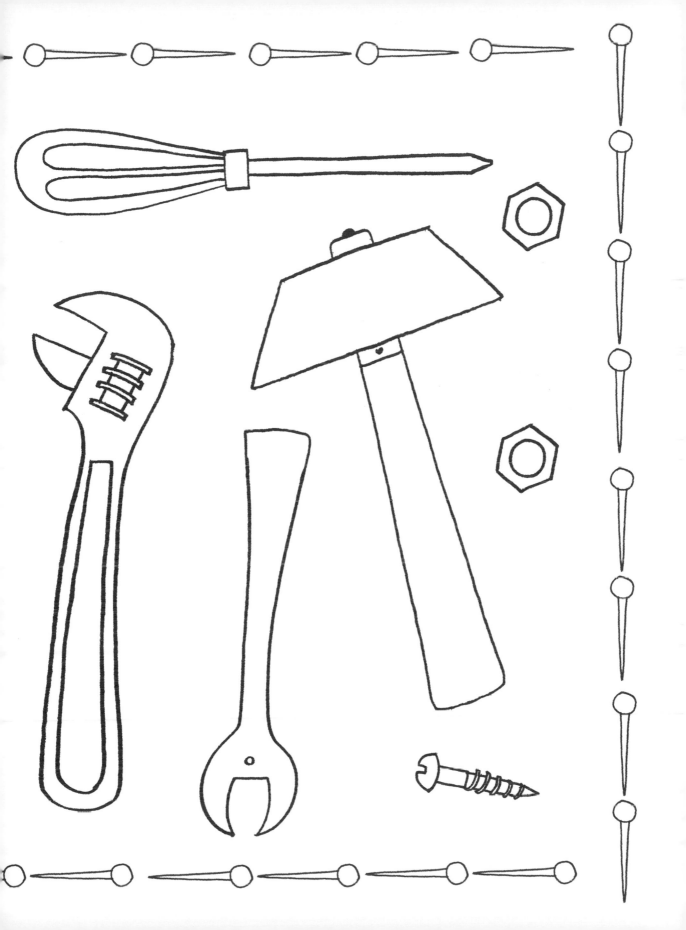

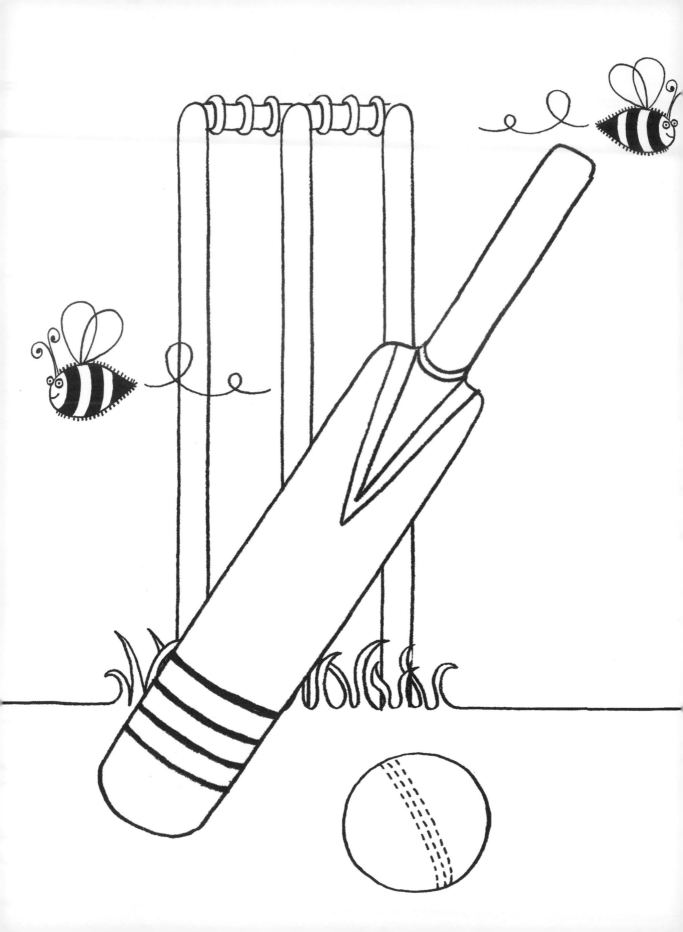

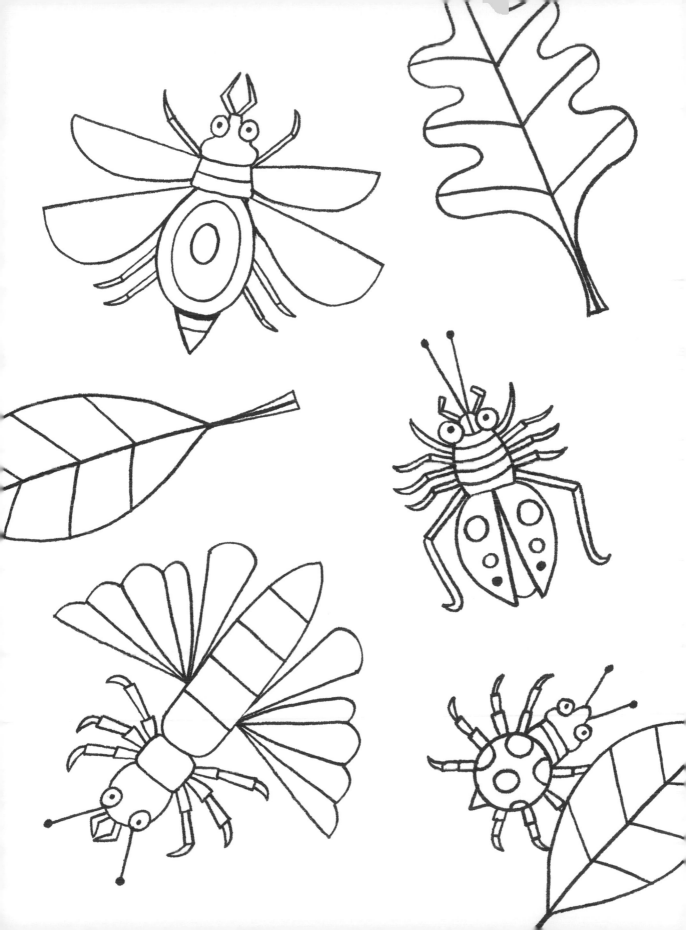

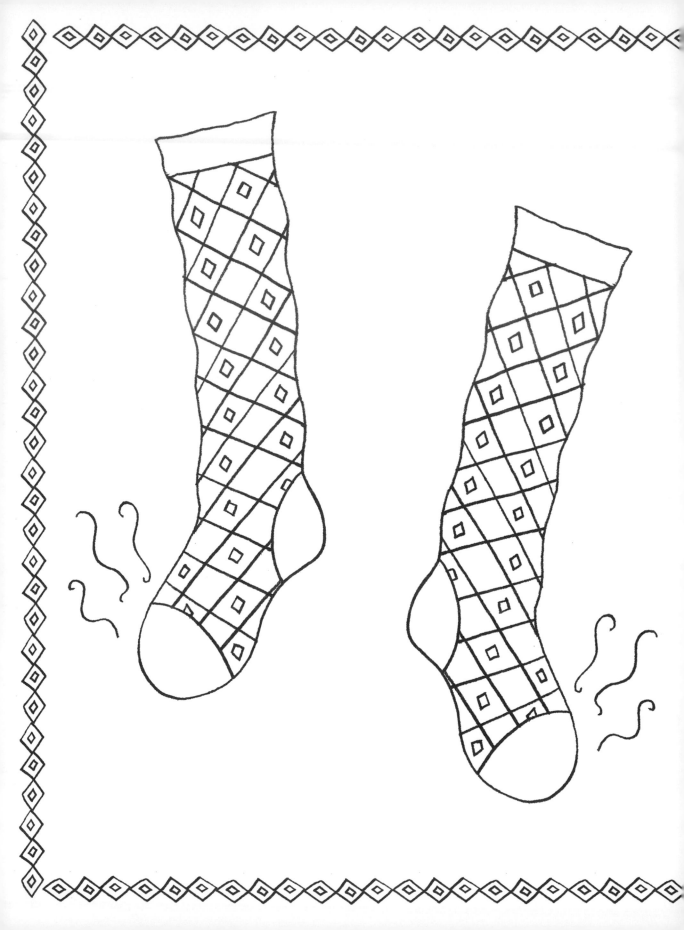

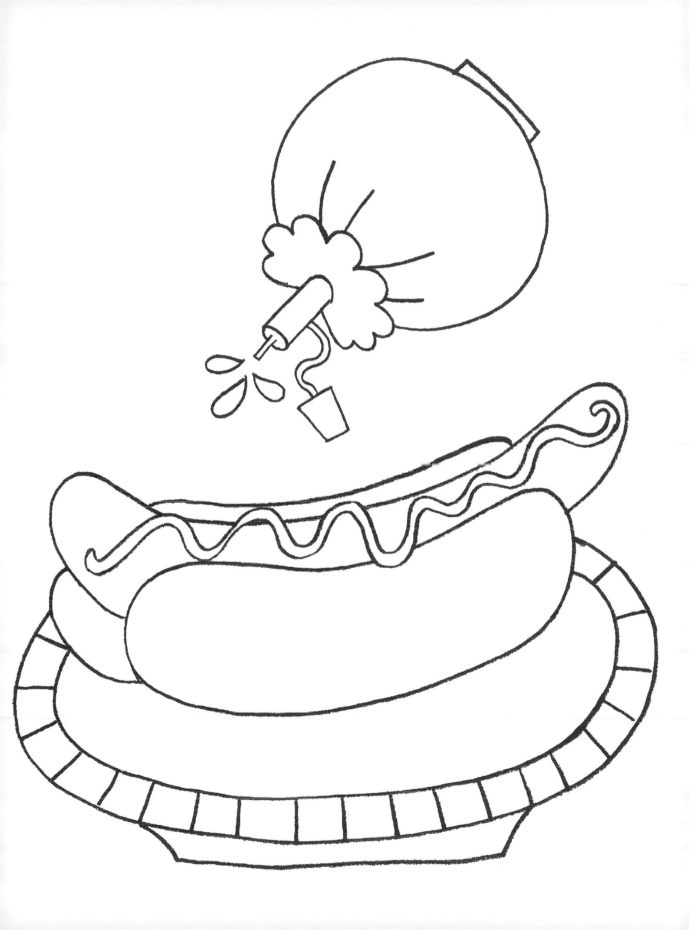

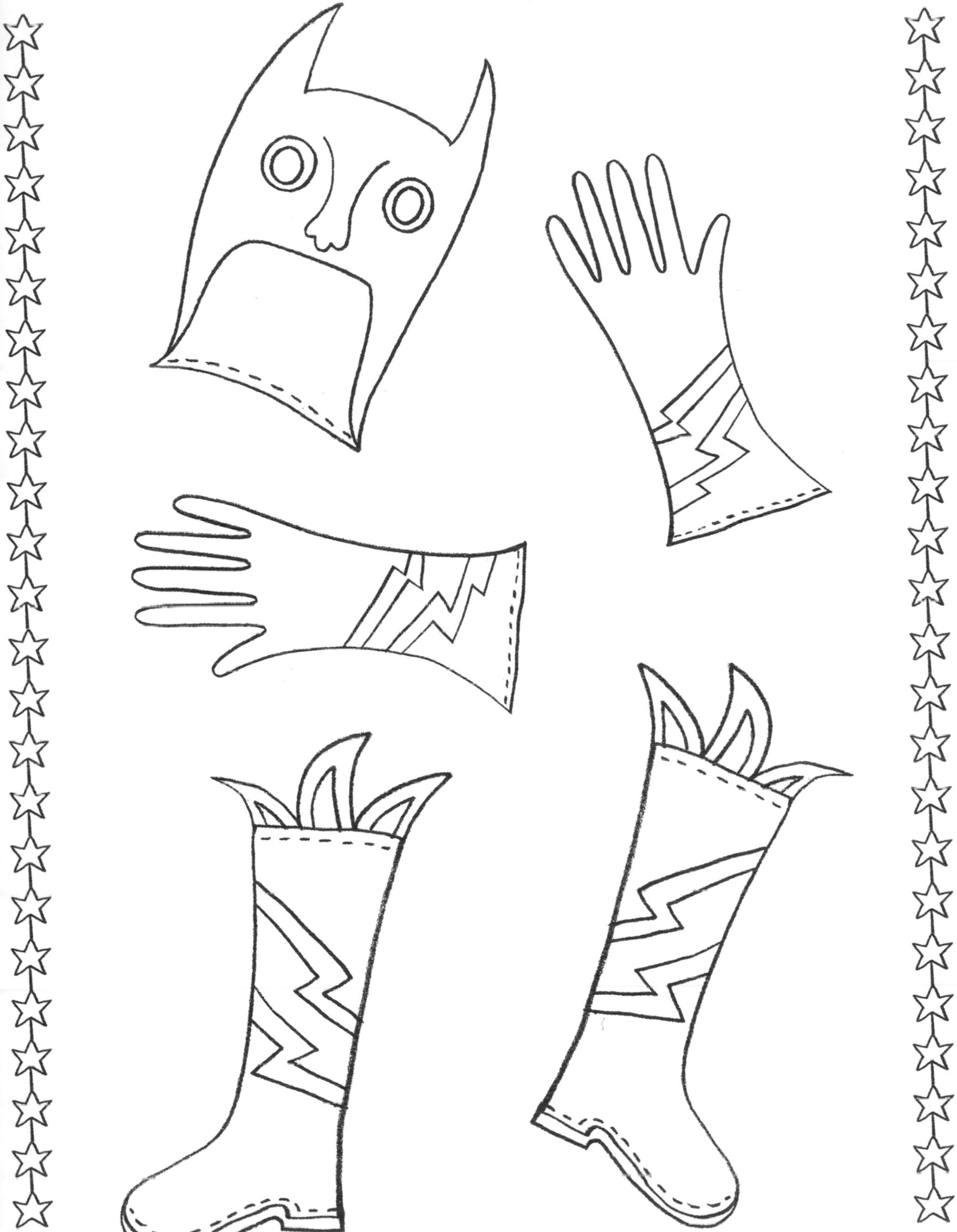

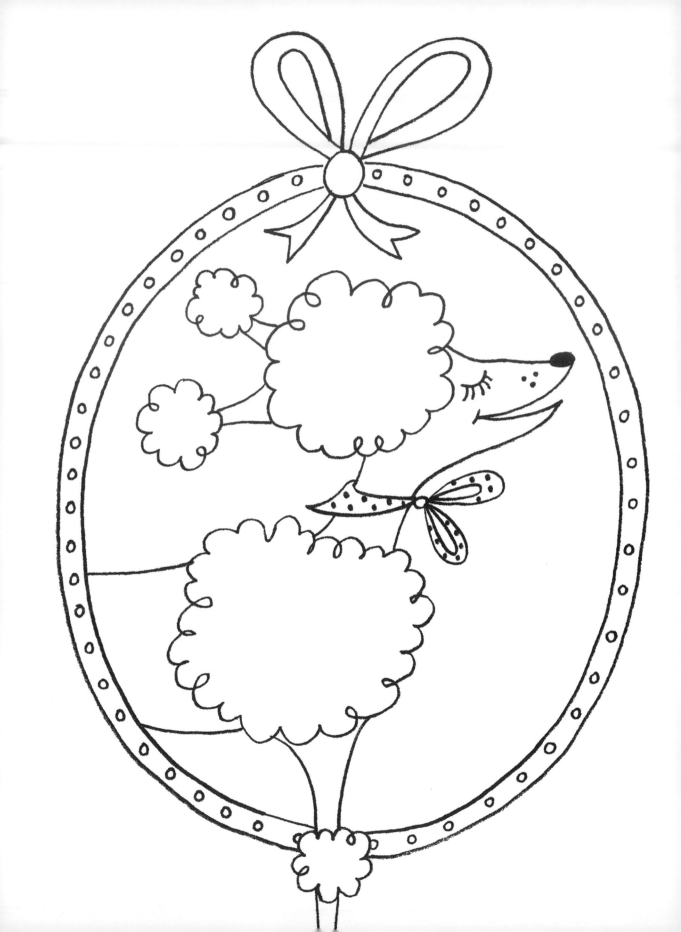

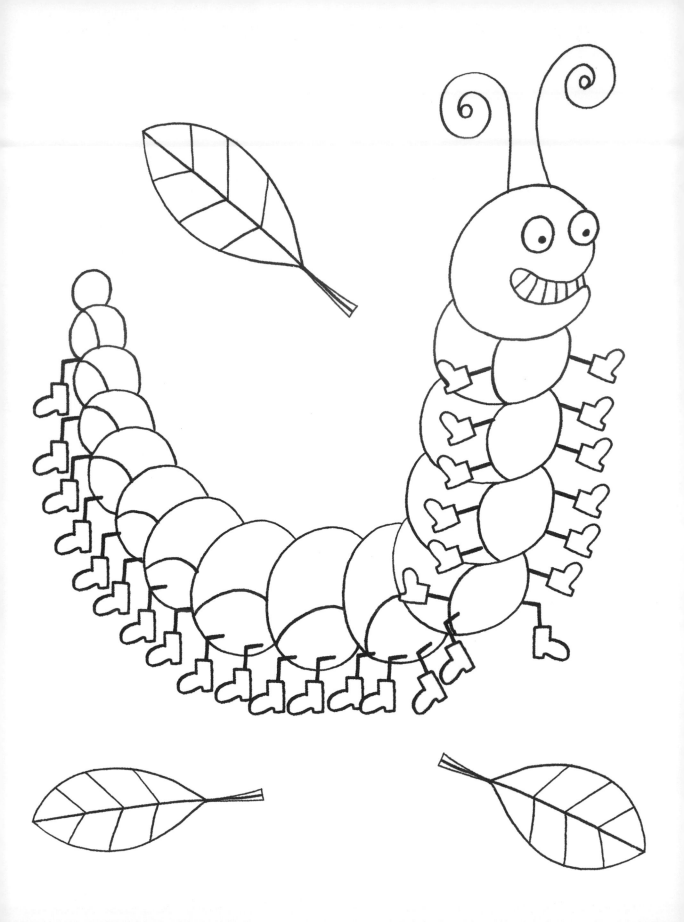

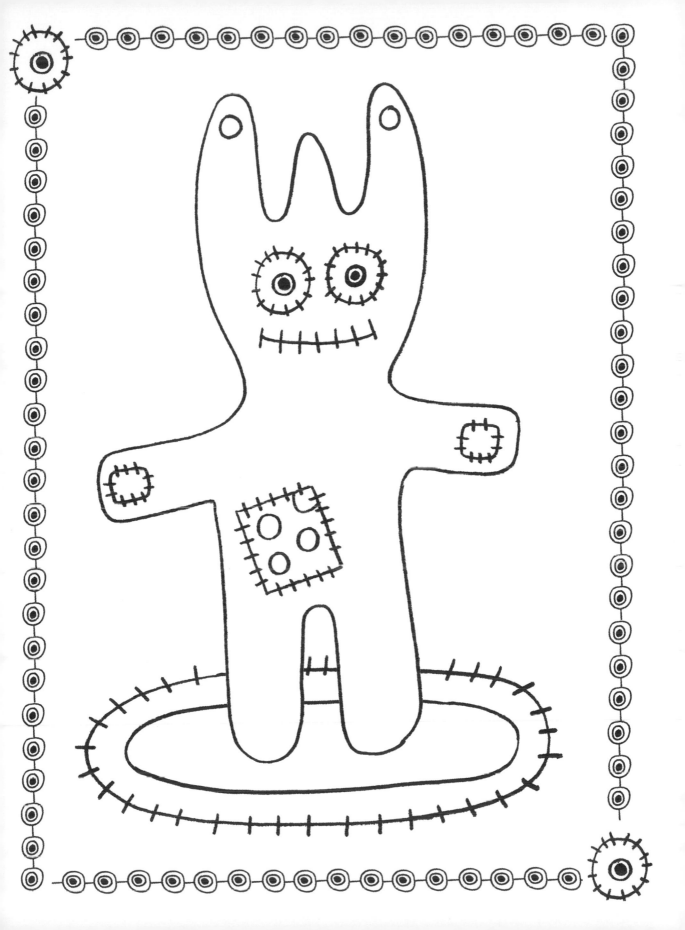

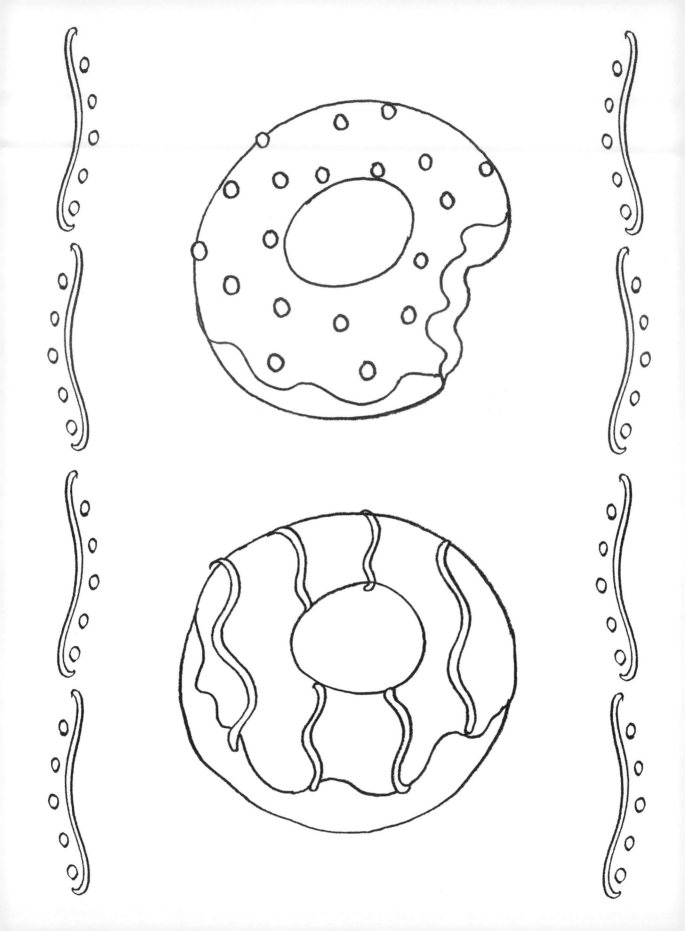

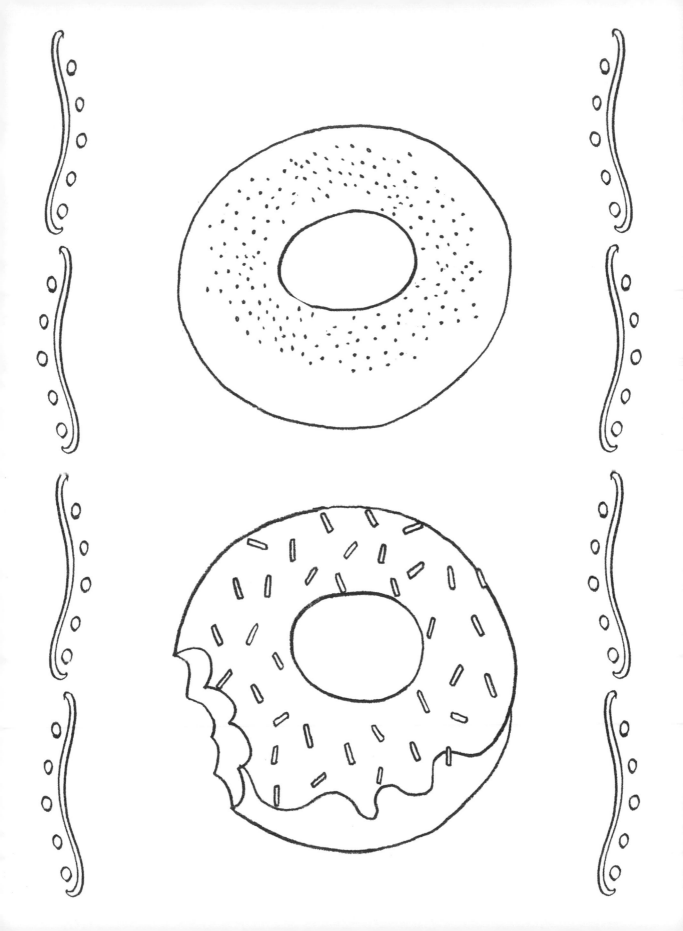